TO LIVE AGAIN

An Advent journey using the
Christmas classic,
IT'S A WONDERFUL LIFE

SHEILA JACOBS

DARTON · LONGMAN + TODD

First published in Great Britain in 2017 by
Darton, Longman and Todd Ltd
1 Spencer Court
140–142 Wandsworth High Street
London SW18 4JJ

ISBN 978-0-232-53329-3

All scripture quotations are taken from the
New International Version (NIV, 2011),
unless otherwise stated.

A catalogue record for this book is available from
the British Library.

Designed and produced by Judy Linard
Printed and bound by Imak Offset, Turkey

CONTENTS

INTRODUCTION

It's that time of year again! How do you feel about it? Be honest! Is Christmas a time of celebrating the birth of the Saviour, of waiting for the coming King? Is it a time of gratitude for the age-old story of shepherds hearing 'peace on earth' from heavenly visitors? A time of joyful expectation of twinkling lights on a 'proper' tree and a table groaning with festive delights, yet plenty of cash left over for the January sales? Mulled wine and carols by candlelight? Snow? Happy and contented relatives?

No?

Is your experience more a hope that the money won't run out, and the kids won't notice the expensive present they really wanted hasn't appeared? Are you worried about getting the right size turkey, sending cards, buying food? Are you *really* irritated by next door's constantly flashing garden lights? Are you expecting a lot of pressure over the holidays with people you rarely see and frankly, don't get on with?

Well, to be truthful, probably a mixture of all the above – right?

We have such high expectations of the Christmas period. The way Christmas is portrayed in the media might go a long way to explain this. It's all such a mix-up of carols and Santa and reindeers and stars and shepherds and commerce. For some reason many of us seem to think we need to supply the 'perfect' Christmas. But what is the perfect Christmas? Something we see in movies? Something that we half-remember from our childhood? For many of us, the season seems to promise so much – and often fails to live up to it. I suspect a lot of us are glad when it's over.

Rather than getting caught up in all the hassle surrounding what can be the most exciting, but most stressful, time of the year, why not take some time to remember what Christmas is *truly* all about? I'm not talking about the 'Saturnalia' we see all around us – the Christianised Roman festivities that leave Christ out, or relegate him to a 'bit part'. I'm talking about remembering the coming of the one who really does bring us the hope, peace, joy and love that is so often missing from the season.

Advent simply means 'coming' (from the Latin, *adventus*). Yes, we are celebrating the birth of the special child who was born in an outhouse in Bethlehem of a virgin mother. But while we celebrate his birth, the season of Advent calls us to looks beyond this. It looks to another coming. The Second Coming of the King of kings. The carpenter from Nazareth who was nailed to a cross for the sins of the world is actually the King of Glory. Revelation tells us of this awesome figure who meets with the apostle John and says: 'Do not be afraid. I am the First and the Last. I am the Living One; I was dead, and now look, I am alive for ever and ever! And I hold the keys of death and Hades' (Revelation 1:17,18). This is the one we are celebrating. This is the one we are waiting for.

This is the one we need to set aside some time to think about and reflect upon during the run-up to the day itself. True, it is the busiest of seasons to find a quiet space to seek the presence of God. But I think we will be blessed if we do.

What better way to engage with God at this time of year than to sit down and watch a favourite Christmas movie and perhaps draw out themes that will help us draw closer to the King of kings?

The film I have chosen to base this Advent journey upon is that perennial Christmas favourite, Frank Capra's *It's a Wonderful Life*, released in 1946, starring James Stewart and Donna Reed. Nominated for five Academy Awards, it's a film all the family can enjoy. You are probably familiar with the popular story. George Bailey (James Stewart) has longed to get away from the small town of Bedford Falls ever since he was a child. But life has had a habit of thwarting his dreams of travel and fulfilment. Every time it seems that George may be able to get away, something happens to put a stop to his hope for freedom. George always does 'the right thing'; he chooses to put other people before his own desires. He marries the girl who has loved him since childhood, Mary (Donna Reed), and settles down in a large, draughty old house that he doesn't like, having a family of four children, still running the business he has had to take over from his father, the Bailey Brothers' Building and Loan. He supplies affordable housing to people who would otherwise live in slum properties belonging to an unpleasant landlord, the villain of the piece, Henry F. Potter (Lionel Barrymore), who owns most of the town – except for George's business. The crisis occurs when at Christmas-time, money goes missing from the Building and Loan – misplaced by the eccentric Uncle Billy (Thomas Mitchell), and hidden by the unscrupulous Potter, who knows the damage this will cause to the Baileys' business. This leads to George's ultimate 'snap'; he considers suicide, after begging Potter for help and being told he is worth more dead than alive.

At this point, help comes as an answer to George's – and others' – prayers. It comes in the shape of Angel Second Class, Clarence Odbody (we will address the whole issue of who angels really are, as we journey through this book!). Clarence jumps into the river, forcing George to rescue him rather than kill himself. Clarence shows George just what life would have been like if he, George, had never been born. Life would have been very different indeed for the people of Bedford Falls, and beyond. George's revelation of the importance and precious nature of his 'wonderful' life means he desperately wants 'to live again' and cries out to God. His life is restored to him, as he sees how very valuable he is, and how his life has worked out for his good, and for everyone else's.

This is a story that can touch us deeply. Just as Christmas can promise so much and often deliver so little, our own lives, especially as we get older, can take on a bittersweet element as we consider dreams we had when we were younger that never came to pass; disappointments perhaps in career, health, relationships. Maybe we, like George, longed to do something great but feel we have settled for the mundane, everyday life we have been dealt; circumstances we would not have chosen; a life for which we may not be actually very grateful.

It's a Wonderful Life has the ability to make us re-evaluate our own situations, and perhaps be thankful for the people we know, the place we live, our jobs, and everything that shapes our lives. More than that, it can make us realise how very valuable we are; how one life can touch so many others. Will we touch them for good, or for bad? There's a challenge for us.

It's also a real challenge for those of us who have started a journey with Jesus. We have believed in him as the one who came to earth to take the punishment we deserve for our personal rebellion against God. He came to restore us to right relationship with our heavenly Father, an eternal relationship, and one that can be rewarding and fulfilling right now, whatever our earthly situation. As we learn to stay in his presence, filled with his Spirit, we will find that hope and peace, and the joy that isn't dependent on our outward circumstances; and a love that is bubbling up within us, God's own love, for the person in front of us. God calls us to trust him; trust him with a life that might not be our 'Plan A' but is his, if we have surrendered our lives to him.

Sometimes I think when we come to Christ we expect him to tick all the boxes we require, but it isn't like that. Following Jesus, being his disciple, is about carrying out *his* will, not ours, just as he did his Father's will (see Luke 22:42). To follow Jesus, we need to look at his life. How did he live? He spent a lot of time with his Father and didn't have his own agenda. Perhaps to us he says: 'Go and do likewise.'

So – whether you know Jesus, are getting to know him, are interested in him, or simply love the film we are watching, my prayer is that at the end of this Advent season you will have a new hope in your relationship with your heavenly Father;

you will know peace with God, available as we receive his Son as our own personal Saviour and Lord; that you will have a fresh joy in his grace; and new love for him as you perhaps receive his love for you in a new way.

I'm using the film to draw out parallels and thought-provoking responses, and I hope it will be an interesting and enjoyable journey for you. Before you start reading, I suggest you relax and watch the movie. It's available on DVD and I suspect you may already have it on your shelf! If not, borrow it, buy it, invite a few friends round, or view it on your own with some snacks to hand.

This book has been written for individual use, but at the back you will find some ideas for groups, if you feel like sharing the themes of the movie with friends, Christian or non-Christian, or perhaps a house group. There will be times to pause for thought, to look at clips of the film to illustrate points, and at the end of each of the four chapters, you will find ideas for activities, refection and prayer. There's no set time for this; it isn't a 'course'; the four chapters don't have to be read as 'weeks'. Dip into it when you can, and as time allows during this busy season. Use it as part of your quiet time with God, if you feel that's appropriate. If you find you have an extra five or ten minutes you can squeeze into your day, to chill out with a cup of coffee and this book, then watch a clip, read the 'Think about' comment and pause for thought. (You don't have to watch the suggested clips – but it might help your Advent journey if you do.) The Advent themes of hope, peace, joy and love are threaded throughout the book.

And this Christmas, may you rediscover, as you read, what a wonderful life we have been given. May you discover a fresh perspective on your own life and situation. I especially pray that if you are feeling discouraged or despondent, disappointed or simply weary, this book will make you want 'to live again' as you experience the hope, peace, joy and love found in Jesus.

Sheila Jacobs
Halstead, Essex

CHAPTER ONE

HOPES AND DREAMS

PREPARE YOURSELF!
What did you want to be, growing up? Did you become (or do you still hope to become) that doctor, writer, accountant, astronaut, mum that you always wanted to be? Or has life taken a different turn? How do you feel about your childhood dreams and ambitions now?

TO START
Right at the beginning of this wonderful film we see that at Christmas-time, prayers are being sent up to heaven for a man called George Bailey. All those people he has helped throughout his life, his wife, his mother and his children, are all praying. Because George is in trouble.

Heaven receives the prayer. And help is on its way. Clarence Odbody, Angel Second

Class, is George's guardian angel. And he is about to be sent on a mission.

Before we go any further, I think right at the start we should look at the issue of who and what angels are. Here, Christianity and the film see things rather differently! The prayers of the people are received in heaven, but not by God. It appears they are received by 'Joseph', a senior angel, and that angels themselves – as in the case of Clarence – are people who have died, and who are waiting to 'earn their wings'.

Have you ever heard people say that when they go to heaven, they will become an angel? Or that someone who died has 'become an angel'? This is not what the Bible teaches. The word 'angel' means 'messenger', and unlike God, they have not always been in existence. Colossians 1:16-17 teaches that Jesus is the creator of all things: 'For in him [Jesus] all things were created: things in heaven and on earth, visible and invisible, whether thrones or powers or rulers or authorities; all things have been created through him and for him. He is before all things, and in him all things hold together.' So Jesus created angels, as a fixed number, and a hierarchy within it. No one *becomes* an angel. These messengers praise God (see Psalm 148:2 – and in the book of Revelation). They do not accept worship (Revelation 22:9) for that belongs only to the triune God. They are sent to help people – but look at this; they are 'ministering spirits sent to serve those who will inherit salvation' (Hebrews 1:14). They specifically help believers in Jesus. Hebrews 13:2 also tells us how they may appear: 'Do not forget to show hospitality to strangers, for by so doing some people have shown hospitality to angels without knowing it.' This would suggest that sometimes we simply can't recognise them from human beings. But they are not human. Jesus described them as quite different: Mark 12:25, for example, tells us: 'When the dead rise, they will neither marry nor be given in marriage; they will be like the angels in heaven.' But *like* doesn't imply we *become* them. Hebrews 9:27 informs us that we are destined 'to die once, and after that to face judgment'. We don't show up in heaven and spend hundreds of years winning our wings. Salvation is found in Jesus Christ, who tells us that he alone is the way to God (see John 14:6), the resurrection and the life (John 11:25).

So, although we know that this is an insertion of fantasy, let's remember that heaven does hear our prayers. And just as we don't become angels, neither do we pray to them (later, Clarence calls out for help from Joseph). Jesus makes it clear that we ourselves can come to the Father, through him, and ask in his name (John 16:26-27).

The 'angels' in this story are having a discussion as a result of prayers received; George Bailey is 'thinking seriously of throwing away God's greatest gift' – his life. Clarence is going to be sent to help. But first, he is taken back to the beginning of George's life. From that, he – and we – can see how George arrived at the point of suicide.

Pause for thought: Think about your ideas of heaven. Do they line up with what's in the Bible?

WATCH: 03:49-3:54

George is a boy, playing with his friends. They are sledging down the snow onto an ice-covered pond, but George's younger brother, Harry, slides straight into frozen water. George saves his brother's life, but it costs him the hearing in his left ear.

THINK ABOUT

Although this episode cost George his hearing, it is immensely relevant, as we see at the end of the story.

Sometimes, even if we have been Christians a long time, we can make spectacular errors of judgement; we can make mistakes; we can turn away from God, even briefly; in short, we sin. It can be that at times it is like skating near thin ice. There may be a sign on an icy pond warning 'Thin ice!' or even 'No skating allowed'. It can be like that in life. We choose to ignore God's warnings – don't go there; don't do it; if you do, the outcome won't be good. It's only when we've had an icy dip and perhaps are recovering that we can see that God warns us for our benefit. He is not a cosmic killjoy. He loves us, and he knows what's best for us.

Like Harry, when we cry out for help, God comes to our rescue. But there's a cost. For George, a deaf ear. For Jesus, the cross.

Pause for thought: Have you ever done a 'good deed' for someone, or perhaps even poured yourself out in love for someone, only to find that it has cost you a great deal? Do you regret helping/loving that person?

Let's come to young George's second good deed.

WATCH: 06:13-11:09

This is a key scene in the film. George has an after-school job in a drugstore – and Mr Gower, the owner, drunk and grieving the loss of his son, mistakenly puts poison into capsules that are meant to be taken by a boy with diphtheria. George notices the error, and although he initially receives a very un-PC response from Mr Gower, invokes the old man's gratitude as he realises what could have happened if the capsules had been administered.

George has run to ask his father what he should do. That is an intriguing little aside. When we're stuck for an answer, when we don't know what to do, why not ask our heavenly Father? Sometimes I think we believe our prayers do land up in some kind of cosmic 'out there' to be picked up by any random angels ... but they are received by God himself. Our heavenly Father loves us, and knows our needs before we ask him. He is always wise, always knows best – and his ideas are not always ours. I believe we also tend to view him as we might have viewed our earthly dads. So, for example, if your father was absent, or distant, that can be how God can seem. But he isn't like that. Jesus came to show us what God is actually like. Walking the dusty roads of Israel, often tired, and hungry, Jesus came to live among us as one of us. He gets it. He understands.

THINK ABOUT
These two episodes could have made young George very bitter and unhappy. He could have been an angry, unforgiving boy, but we see here that he is very cheerful, outgoing and friendly, whistling happily. A local girl, Mary – and another girl, Violet – both appear to have crushes on him. George, in the second scene, shares with Mary some of his dreams regarding travel. He has great plans, even from an early age!

Sometimes, things that happen to us

can leave us understandably bitter and unforgiving. One of the biggest problems, in my view – and in my own personal experience – is that unforgiveness can block the presence of God.

Jesus spoke a great deal about forgiveness. In Matthew 6 we read the Lord's Prayer, in which we are encouraged to forgive others as we ourselves have been forgiven. Jesus adds: 'For if you forgive other people when they sin against you, your heavenly Father will also forgive you. But if you do not forgive others their sins, your Father will not forgive your sins' (verses 14-15). That's quite a thought, isn't it? We all sin. We all need to be forgiven. If we say we haven't sinned, we are deceiving ourselves, as 1 John 1:8 tells us. Romans 3:23 says: 'for all have sinned and fall short of the glory of God'. That's *all* of us, me and you. Our sins – things we have done and said and simply are – have separated us from God and from one other. That's why we need a Saviour. We can't save ourselves. Only a perfect man can pay the price for sinful humankind. And only God could live that perfect life required of God, that eternal life, and lay it down for us.

Pause for thought: It has been said that not forgiving another person is like drinking poison and expecting the person who hurt you to die. How true do you think that is?

WATCH: 15:46-17:30

Moving on in the film, we see George, grown up, still hoping to travel and get away from small-town Bedford Falls. His brother has just graduated from high school, and George is going to go travelling and then to college. He has been helping run the Bailey Brothers' Building and Loan Association and the plan is that when he returns from college, Harry will then go. George wants to build things, design buildings – he has great ambition. He really doesn't want to be 'cooped up for the rest of my life in a shabby little office' ... he wants to do 'something big, something important'. But his gracious father believes the Building and Loan *are* doing something important – helping poor people to buy their own properties (and not making much money in the process). They are enabling people to get out of the malevolent Mr Potter's slums. Mr Potter is now on the board of directors of the Building and Loan, but in truth, as we see later on, he wants it ruined – or to own it. It is the only thing he doesn't own in the town.

George goes off to Harry's party, and meets up with Mary again. There is obviously an attraction there, and they dance together.

Walking home, having changed clothes due to an accident with a swimming pool (watch that bit later!), they come across an old house that Mary says she would love to live in one day. But George's wishes are quite different …

WATCH: 24:40-25:43; 28:12-26

Both the above scenes show us clearly that George Bailey has no intention of staying in Bedford Falls. He is full of excitement about his future. He tells Mary of his intentions to see the world. He has great plans. He knows what he's going to do tomorrow, the next day, next year, year after that: 'I'm shaking the dust of this crummy little town off my feet and I'm going to see the world!' he says … He'll go to college, then he'll build things … All George's plans fade into the background, though, as he finds out his father has had a stroke.

Life has conspired against him. Or maybe it is working out for his good – and for the good of other people too. He just can't see it yet.

THINK ABOUT

Sometimes life doesn't seem to pan out the way we think it ought, or that we hoped for. But maybe, just maybe, if we have committed our way to God, it is the way *he* has planned. Our great dreams may not have worked out – yet – perhaps there are some we are still waiting on for their fulfilment. Can we trust God to work them out as he wants? It's a case of trusting him.

Pause for thought: Have you asked God about his plans for you? Do you believe God's plans are good, and personal?

WATCH: 28:43-32:26

George's father has died, and George has given up his trip to Europe to help out at the Building and Loan. Mr Potter wants to dissolve the company – of course. Mr Potter attacks George's father's business practices and his character, and George gives an impassioned response. The upshot is, the board vote Potter down but on one condition: George takes his father's place as Executive Secretary. If he doesn't do it … they'll vote with Potter.

And so George misses his chances of travel and college and getting away. He does the right thing. All his dreams are sliding out of his grasp.

THINK ABOUT

Has that ever been your experience? Or have you had your dreams fulfilled? Sometimes the longing for them doesn't match up to the achievement. What do I mean by that? Well – we might think something in particular will fulfil our longing. Perhaps we want to marry, get that job, go that place, and we want it so much it becomes almost an idol. It takes over our heart; it takes over the place of God. God has made a 'void' inside each one of us that can only be filled by him. He made us to love him, and he wants to love us. He is enough for us; all our other desires and longings stem from that paramount relationship with him. No relationship, job, holiday or material possession can fill that longing. It might satisfy for a while; but before long, we may find that it isn't really what we're looking for. Only God himself can ultimately fill the void.

> *Pause for thought: Have you ever been in a situation that you feel you can't get out of? Are you in that position now?*

ADVENT CONNECTION

READ: JOHN 1:1-18

Jesus, the exact representation of the living God – God in a body (see Hebrews 1:3; Colossians 2:9) came to earth that first Christmas, why? To reconcile people to God. He is called 'Emmanuel' in the Christmas story (see Matthew 1:23; Isaiah 7:14) which means: 'God with us'.

With the coming of Jesus, salvation in him isn't just about heaven 'one day', but about a living relationship with a God who loves us *today*. That is the great hope of the world

– light coming into our darkness (see Isaiah 9:2). That God wasn't counting our sins against us (2 Corinthians 5:19), but instead came here in the form of his Son, the second person of the mysterious Trinity, to bring us into relationship with himself. Jesus was the 'Word [made] flesh' who 'made his dwelling among us' (verse 14).

At the start of this film, we see a view of heaven that isn't strictly biblical. People don't die and become angels, earning their wings. Indeed, we can earn nothing. At the first Christmas, the first Advent, God became Man for us, to save us from an eternity without him. He doesn't want anyone to live apart from him (see John 3:16).

I had a friend who died in her forties. One lady told me that my friend 'was in heaven' and I said yes, I believed she was, because she had asked Jesus into her life before she died. 'Oh no,' this lady responded, quite shocked. 'Lucy [not her real name] wasn't into religion. But we *all* go to heaven!' I believe that is a deluded thought, sadly. Humanity rejected God (see Genesis 3). After our rebellion, we were separated from our holy, righteous God, and we can't get right with him on our own. We can't work to earn salvation, or our 'wings' once we die. All our good works, says the Bible, are as 'filthy rags' in his sight (Isaiah 64:6). Even someone as good and kind as Peter Bailey, while making a remarkable difference on earth, could not earn their way into heaven! Does this seem fair? Well, yes. Our good deeds can't cancel out our bad ones. There isn't a cosmic weighing scale. It isn't about deeds, as such. It is about *who we are*. We are by very nature 'sinners'. That is why it is so wonderful that Jesus came, while we were still God's enemies – yes, enemies, that's what the New Testament says (Romans 5:10) – to save us. Only he could. And he did. Why? Because he loves us.

Ephesians 2:8-9 sums it up: 'For it is by grace you have been saved, through faith – and this is not from yourselves, it is the gift of God – not by works, so that no one can boast.' And what's 'grace'? God's free, unmerited favour – for you and for me.

The wonderful thing about Advent is that it was God's plan from the start to send his Son. We see in the Old Testament prophecies about the hope of his coming:

For to us a child is born,
to us a son is given,
and the government will be on his shoulders.

And he will be called
Wonderful Counsellor, Mighty God,
Everlasting Father, Prince of Peace.

(Isaiah 9:6)

'But you, Bethlehem Ephrathah,
Though you are little among the thousands
   of Judah,
Yet out of you shall come forth to Me
The One to be Ruler in Israel,
Whose goings forth *are* from of old,
From everlasting.'

(Micah 5:2, NKJV)

'Therefore the Lord himself will give you a
sign: the virgin will conceive and give birth
to a son, and will call him Immanuel.'

(Isaiah 7:14)

How wonderful that the Light of the World
has come into our darkness, into our broken
dreams and disappointments, difficulties
and hardships!

Pause for thought
- Has anything in your life – or
  anyone – caused you to feel bitter
  or resentful? Can you bring that

to Jesus today, knowing he won't condemn you, but will set you free?

- There's a saying that is attributed to Edmund Burke: 'The only thing necessary for the triumph of evil is for good men to do nothing.' Do you think that's true? What do you think that means for people who know they have been forgiven by Jesus and are right with God?

ACTIVITY SUGGESTIONS:

- It could be that this chapter has made you rethink some of your ideas about God, about Jesus, about heaven, and about 'works'. If you feel you've been challenged on your own personal faith, why not talk to a trusted church leader, or Christian friend?

- Is there anyone you need to forgive? Judgement says 'you must pay'; mercy says 'but I will forgive you'; grace says 'and I will do you good you don't deserve'. God has done this for us, in Jesus. Can you extend grace to somebody this Christmas?

REFLECTION:

We can do good works, but it won't make us right with God. That's why Jesus has come into the world. Rather than being hopeless, knowing we can't get rid of our own sinful natures, we can trust him, once we come to him, to make us new and clean and different. Jesus said we only had to ask him and he would give us 'living water' that is the Holy Spirit, living inside us (see John 4:10,14). Have you asked him for this gift? Light an Advent Candle or put on some worship music/Christmas carols, and give glory to God!

PRAYER

Father God, thank you so much for sending your Son, Jesus, into the world. Thank you that you hear and respond to prayers; that you care about us. Lord, thank you that you want us to be in relationship with you. Help me, as I read through this little book, to really meet with you and hear what you are saying to me. Amen.

CHAPTER TWO
WHEN LIFE DOESN'T GO OUR WAY

PREPARE YOURSELF!

Do you have a 'bucket list'? It can be as simple as watching fireworks with someone you love (that was one of mine) to going to the other side of the world, writing a novel, becoming self-employed, entering the ministry ... the list is endless! If there are things you'd like to do that seem impossible, bring them to God now. Ask him if they are his ideas. If they aren't, ask him to give you better ones – plans that he will bring to pass.

TO START

In this section, we see how grown-up George makes choices that lead to an even closer connection with Bedford Falls. He didn't intend to stay there; life just seems to make the decision for him. It's strange how that happens, isn't it? People say that our lives are determined by our choices, but I haven't always found that to be so. Sometimes we are very much affected by the choices *other people* make, or purely due to the fact that 'stuff happens'.

In my young adulthood, what I didn't plan for was becoming ill. I started to experience severe dizzy spells and by my late thirties I was diagnosed with what they said was Ménière's disease. Severely agoraphobic – mostly terrified by the illness – I couldn't work, couldn't even attend church, and lived with my mum. That was not in my 'Plan A'.

God is gracious though, and opened doors for me to become an author of children's fiction, and later, books for adults (yes, this is one of them). I became a full-time editor of Christian books and magazines, my health began to improve drastically and today I am living a normal life, with good health and at the time of writing am privileged to be serving as a deacon in my church. When I was ill, this wasn't something I thought I would ever be able to do.

So, like most people, I have had a speckled

journey. Not one I had planned, and yet one that has proved rich – certainly in terms of my relationship with Jesus. My years of isolation proved to be a time of laying a deep foundation with God. I don't believe I would have become a writer and editor without God's intervention and guidance.

Looking at George Bailey's life, as we will shortly, we can see that his own plans disintegrate into dust as life moves on. Is George a Christian? Well, we don't see him consulting God – except in desperation. This film was made at a time when faith in God was more of a norm, especially in the USA. Prayer seems, then, more natural when we come to it later on in the film.

What George doesn't see, at this stage, is how he is building a solid life and affecting so many other people for good!

Pause for thought: Are you able to thank God for choices he may have stopped you from making?

WATCH: 34.00-36:13; 37:17-38:19
In the first clip we see Harry coming back from college, four years later. George has

sent his brother to school, and has stayed home to run the business. Harry has done well; he has become a 'football star'. He has also married.

George hopes, of course, that Harry will take over the business he has been running so that George can now get away and travel – fulfilling his dreams. But Ruth's father has offered Harry a good job in research …

The expression on George's face tells all in this clip. The actor, James Stewart, who died in 1997, having been born in 1908 – really had a gift of portraying innermost emotions, without having to say a word. Although we may have to suspend belief in some of the earlier scenes that he looks young enough to go to college – he was obviously pushing forty at this point! – he manages to display the emotions of the older George incredibly well.

In the second clip, I noticed how George doesn't complain to his brother, or start shouting, 'It's not fair.' Although he does mention, rather bitterly, to his mother that the new wife will be keeping Harry out of Bedford Falls!

The longing in his face as he hears the train pull away is very emotive. It's symbolic of his dreams leaving town … and he throws away the literature he has been cherishing, promising an enticing new life far away. His mother then talks to him about Mary, who is 'back from school'. She says Mary will 'help you find the answers'.

THINK ABOUT

How good are you at expressing your emotions? Do you keep things bottled up? Are there people you trust with whom you can share your innermost thoughts? Can another person help us find life's answers? At times we may believe another person can fill that void in us that I mentioned earlier, the gap that actually only God can fill. But we can be of assistance to others, especially if we know Jesus.

My granny was used by God to point me to Jesus. She spoke about him, but there was also something *different* about her. As we live close to Jesus, his fragrance will surround us: 'But thanks be to God, who always leads us as captives in Christ's triumphal procession and uses us to spread the aroma of the knowledge of him everywhere. For we are to God the pleasing aroma of Christ among those who are being saved and those who are perishing. To the one we are an aroma that brings death; to the other, an aroma that brings life ...' (2 Corinthians 2:14–16). As we are continually filled by his Spirit, he will 'leak out of us'. This is the important thing: to live in his presence, aware of him, 'remaining' in him as Jesus spoke about in John 15.

So we need to point people to the one who really does have all the answers. We may not understand some of them, but that's where faith comes in. When I had to put my mother, who has dementia and Parkinson's disease, into a care home, I remember asking God about it and having the reply: 'I'm in it with you.' This is something that I have found to be true. There is a whole world out there that doesn't know that God is a God who so loves them that he sent his Son to save them. So many people think that God is harsh – if he does exist – and are ready to blame such a God for all the woes on the planet. Isn't it interesting how people expect or suspect that God is malevolent, not good? There's so much evil in the world, after all. But we are living with the result of rebellion against our Creator, and we have an enemy, too – the accuser, or Satan. Dark forces are at work in the world and that is plain to see.

But this is the time of year when we are

remembering that God sent his Son into the darkness to set us free. If we know we have the answer – in Jesus – how can we best help others to see what we have found, and to point them in the right direction?

Pause for thought: Is there someone in your life who needs to be gently pointed towards Jesus?

WATCH: 39:48-40:44

Here, we see an interesting little encounter between George and the rather racy Violet. Yes, George is 'tired of just reading about things' – but one wonders what is on Violet's mind; possibly not travel! However, when he suggests his idea of a wild time to the wild girl, she doesn't understand at all. To me, she seems a picture of the carnal mind.

THINK ABOUT

George has higher, exciting ideas. Violet's ideas seem to centre around relationships. So many people are like this today, both in and out of the church. I think sometimes people look at relationships as a kind of 'cure-all', and simply cannot be alone. But men and women are not designed to be each other's Saviour. Although a good relationship can be a blessing, we shouldn't make the other person (or the longed-for person, if we are not married) our idol. Violet reminds me very much of the woman at the well (see John 4). Jesus spoke to her about her serial relationships, but then told her that if she had asked him, he would give her 'living water' which would mean she would never thirst again, and would 'become in [her] a spring of water welling up to eternal life' (verse 14). He is of course referring to the Spirit of God. Only God truly fulfils – we may be blessed with good marriages and fine friendships, but that inner 'empty' we all know is God-made for God to fill.

George is looking for something greater, something beautiful, something beyond his mediocre, boring life. But it isn't found in travel or jobs or relationships. Ultimately it is found in relationship with God through Jesus Christ.

Pause for thought: Have you asked Jesus to give you the living water?

WATCH: 41:39-48:06

That Mary has been in love with George all along is quite evident – she obviously wants to settle down with him. Here we see the huge power of romantic attraction, culminating in George's intense speech. Mary uses another 'admirer' to provoke a reaction in George. And it works. Her proximity is too much for him. He is trying to resist her charms – he doesn't want to get married.

The culmination is after he has been offered to get into a business deal by his old friend Sam Wainwright – incidentally, he makes a suggestion regarding a new factory that Sam's family intends to build elsewhere – why not locate it in Bedford Falls? Even in this, he is doing good by providing work for the locals who lost their jobs when the old tool and machinery works was closed down. Even this 'chance of a lifetime' isn't one that George wants to take – although it would mean he'd get away from the Building and Loan, at least!

He says to Mary, as he grabs her and tells her he doesn't want to get married to anyone, ever: 'I want to do what I want to do!'

THINK ABOUT
1. Lust or love?

I'm sure I don't need to tell you that sexual attraction is a very powerful thing! Proverbs 4:23 tells us to guard our hearts, because everything we do flows out from it. In fact, Jesus himself said in Luke 6:45: 'A good man brings good things out of the good stored up in his heart, and an evil man brings evil things out of the evil stored up in his heart. For the mouth speaks what the heart is full of.' While it may not always be a thing of the 'heart' but more of the flesh, what we allow to take root in our minds will certainly bear fruit. It's not wise to do anything with someone 'in the mind' that you wouldn't do with them in the flesh. As Christians, we should be treating each other as brothers and sisters unless we are in a marriage relationship.

Marriage is God's idea. Right back in the book of Genesis he said it wasn't good for the man to be alone, and made woman as his companion (2:18). Sadly, relationships seem often to take on the quality of commercialism. How do I mean? Well – if I buy a carpet and in a few years I notice it is a bit worn, a bit dreary, and I'd like something new, I replace it.

But people are not carpets, they are not items. God did not intend people to be rejected or replaced. No one ever said that marriage was easy; in fact, someone once told me: 'It is better never to marry than to marry the wrong person', and there is great merit in staying single (see Paul's teaching in 1 Corinthians 7; also Matthew 19:12) yet, when marriage works it can be beautiful.

Marriage is good. And for a Christian, the option is only ever to be married to another Christian (2 Corinthians 6:14; 1 Corinthians 7:39). If you are already married and your husband or wife is not a Christian, then don't leave them (1 Corinthians 7:12-16). But if you are praying for a spouse, make sure any prospective candidates are believers in Jesus! You need someone you can pull together with. George obviously wanted something other than Mary's hope of a settled existence. I wouldn't say she manipulated him here – but there was certainly a little bit of manoeuvring. Manoeuvring generally isn't a good plan.

Love is free; you can't *make* someone else love you, just as God doesn't *make* us love him; he invites us into relationship. Love that is forced is no love at all.

Pause for thought: What's your heart full of?

2. 'I want to do what I want to do!'

It's worth noting this plaintive cry. I think we have probably all been there at some time or other. Of course we all want to do what we want to do! It's human nature, right from the Garden of Eden – and look what happened there. What we want to do isn't always what's right or good or the best for us or others. If we do 'our own thing' and ignore any warnings, we are probably heading for that icy dip I mentioned earlier. Emotions can lie to us. Feelings can't always be trusted. And although we may enjoy ourselves if we do what 'we want to do' rather than what we know is right or what we know we should be doing, it will more than likely end nowhere good. Sometimes God may challenge us not to go with our feelings, but to go with what *he* is telling us, which might be the exact opposite to what we desire; if we obey him, we put him first and show him that he can trust us ... trust us, perhaps, to do more exploits in his kingdom.

Pause for thought: A track that looks primrose-laden may lead to a sheer drop, whereas a rocky, difficult path may lead to a beautiful beach.

WATCH: 48:48-52:38

Married and heading for a honeymoon in New York and Bermuda, even Mary seems to throw caution to the wind. But the exciting start to the marriage with the promise of a mini getaway soon doesn't transpire. This the time of the Depression and there's a bank run ...

The bank has closed. They have called in the Building and Loan's loan. There's no money left. The people are frightened and are at the Building and Loan, desperate to have funds until the bank opens again ... and then Potter calls.

He has guaranteed the bank sufficient

funds, and they will be closed for a week … in other words, he has taken over the bank. He offers fifty cents on the dollar for anyone who brings their shares to him … and then George sees the sign on the wall: 'All that you can take with you is that which you have given away.'

The greedy Potter character here reminds me of the story Jesus told of the rich man in Luke 12:13-21. He was wealthy already when his land yielded a bumper harvest. He decided to build bigger barns, store his surplus grain, and take life easy. But what he didn't realise was that very night his life would be over: 'You fool!' says God, in verse 20. 'This very night your life will be demanded from you. Then who will get what you have prepared for yourself?'

THINK ABOUT

It's easy to put our trust in wealth when we have it. But when the banks crash, and the pension doesn't materialise, when illness takes our savings – what will we be trusting in then?

Mr Potter seems to have no redeeming characteristics. Throughout the film he doesn't soften at all. With no family and apparently no finer feelings, his heart is as hard as the money he worships. This is what happens when money becomes our idol. We become like what we worship.

What's the point of trusting in money, however much we have? God is Jehovah-Jireh (see Genesis 22:14), our provider, and as we get closer to him, that love will give us the security that we may be trying to find in our finances. I think it's about that a lot of the time, don't you? Our security isn't in God so it's in something else. We can certainly see who we trust by the way we spend our cash – especially when it comes to giving it away. 1 Timothy 6:10 tells us that it is *the love* of money that is 'a root of all kinds of evil'. Money in itself can be used for much good – as we see in the story, as George lends money to people so that they can get out of poverty, living in slums, and own their own properties. But the love and adoration of money can cause many to '[wander] from the faith'.

Pause for thought: What do you think this saying means: 'All that you can take with you is that which you've given away'?

WATCH: 54:23-56:23

This clip features another impassioned speech by George – at a time when everyone is losing their head, he keeps cool and keeps doing good. Galatians 6:9 tells us not to give up doing good ... but that can be hard when we're in a panic. As the people are here.

George saves the Building and Loan and keeps it out of the clutches of Potter, who owns everything else in the town; if Potter gets his hands on the company, there would never be another decent house built in Bedford Falls! Here we see George's heart; he wants to keep the people out of Potter's overpriced slums!

The people are acting out of fear, but George saves the day with his clarity of thought. The money he was going to use for his honeymoon getaway is used instead to save the day.

THINK ABOUT

Panic can make us do things we wouldn't normally do. It's rarely a good idea to act on fear. The Bible is full of exhortations to 'fear not'. Jesus said often, 'Don't be afraid.' (As an exercise, check out the following if you have time: Matthew 10:21; 14:27; 17:7; Mark 5:36; 6:50; Luke 5:10; 8:50; 12:7; John 6:20.)

Fear and panic steal our peace. Just like unforgiveness, they can rob us of the sense of the presence of God. We need to come to Jesus and trust him more so that we can live in a peace that passes understanding, as Philippians 4 teaches. Interestingly, there we can see the way to such peace: 'Rejoice in the Lord always. I will say it again: rejoice! Let your gentleness be evident to all. The Lord is near. Do not be anxious about anything, but in every situation, by prayer and petition, with thanksgiving, present your requests to God. And the peace of God, which transcends all understanding, will guard your hearts and your minds in Christ Jesus' (verses 4-7). It's about giving your anxieties to Jesus. Can you cast all your cares on him, as 1 Peter 5:7 exhorts, whatever they may be – plans for the future, financial worries? Try it. And experience his peace. Remember, 'he cares for you'.

Pause for thought: Are you experiencing anxiety at the moment? What's the root of that anxiety? Trust God.

ADVENT CONNECTION

READ: LUKE 1:26-38; LUKE 2:1-20

In the first reading, we look at the amazing story of the angel Gabriel visiting Mary. He tells her not be afraid (1:30) and gives her astounding news. Then further astounding news for the shepherds on the hillside on the night of Jesus' birth, with yet another admonition to not be afraid (2:10).

Mary had probably grown up with the dreams many girls of her age and culture would have – marriage, children. It wasn't actually so much 'dreams' as the way life was. As a Jewish girl, she was awaiting the advent of the Messiah – but surely she had no idea that God would choose *her* to be involved in such a way.

But Mary didn't lose her cool over this. Her answer to the angel is one of quiet obedience. She clearly loves and trusts God. How would things work out, in a culture that would call for the pregnant, unmarried woman's death? There seems to be no fear here, though. And that amazes me.

Clearly, as her own life plans were radically changed, she said to the angel: 'I am the Lord's servant … May your word to me be fulfilled.' She would have to tell her betrothed, of course – Joseph. In those days, betrothal meant rather more than the kind of engagement we have now in the Western world. It would require a divorce to break it off. I wonder what was really going through Mary's head at this time. And what of Joseph? His plans had gone awry as well. Matthew chapter 1 tells us that he realised Mary was telling the truth after an angelic encounter (see 1:20-21). His world was turned upside down too. He hadn't expected to marry a girl who was pregnant with God's Son! It would mean a flight to Egypt he hadn't anticipated (Matthew 2:13-15).

The shepherds would have had an unexpected interruption to their ordinary lives too – something that would radically change their perspective on life forever. A company of angels appeared to them, singing 'Glory to God in the highest heaven, and on earth peace to those on whom his favour rests' (Luke 2:14). Shepherds were not valued members of society; indeed, they were considered outcasts. But they were chosen to greet the King of kings … the one who came to save outcasts, the rejected, 'sinners' – to tell them that there was a place for them, too, in his kingdom. Surely the shepherds' lives were never the same again!

God calls us into relationship with him – a relationship of peace. Sadly, people fail us, and we fail them, and ultimately they will leave us or we will leave them, whether we want to or not. We can save money, but we can lose it too; and we can't take it with us when we die. Nothing stays the same forever. The peace that God offers is based in something far more permanent than any worldly friendship or security. We have his favour because his Son has made the way for us to be in relationship with God. That which separated us has been taken away – demonstrated by the tearing of the temple curtain as Jesus died (Matthew 27:51).

But following Jesus means surrendering to him, just as Mary surrendered to God. Trusting him, and obeying him, we can avoid making wrong choices, and living in fear. When we realise how much he loves us, we will trust him to take care of us and bring to pass the good plans that he has for us (Jeremiah 29:11). Ephesians 2:10 tells us that 'we are God's handiwork, created in Christ Jesus to do good works, which God prepared in advance for us to do'. In the film, George does good works for the people, and it seems to come naturally to him. He just cares. He's a nice guy. A decent guy. Not at all selfish.

Surrendering our lives to Jesus means we let go, and let God. There's no room for selfishness. When we see what he accomplished for us on the cross, to bring us peace with God, our thankfulness and gratitude should really overflow – especially when we see clearly that as we said before, our good works can't make us right with God; and that, inside, we fall far short of his perfect standard.

Let's say with the apostle Paul – and no doubt with Mary, the angels and the shepherds: 'Thanks be to God for his indescribable gift!' (2 Corinthians 9:15). Thank God for his free favour – his wonderful grace; peace with God forever!

Pause for thought
- Are there any relationships in your life you should let go of? Or any that you need God's help with?

> • The angels spoke of peace – but we don't see that in the world. What kind of peace do you think they were really talking about?

ACTIVITY SUGGESTIONS:

- Pick a character – Mary, Joseph, one of the shepherds. Put yourself into the scene; imagine the starry night, the angelic encounters; the uncertainty, the fear, the excitement. Which part of the Christmas story really speaks to you at this point?

- 'All that you can take with you is that which you have given away.' What can you give away this Christmas, to bless someone?

REFLECTION:

Many things cause us to lose peace. When life seems to 'go wrong', when we feel frustrated or angry, things don't go our way, relationships and friendships falter, and money is tight ... Remember God's favour; his grace – his love for you. Mary trusted

God in a most amazing way; she didn't panic at all. Look at the names of Jesus in Isaiah 9:6. One of them is 'Prince of Peace'. Is there an area in your life where you need peace today?

PRAYER

Father, thank you so much that you are my provider, the Source of my strength, and the one who says, 'Don't fear.' Help me to commit my whole self to you – for you know the plans you have for me, and I believe they are good plans, because you are good, and you love me. Amen.

CHAPTER THREE
IN THE DARK TIMES

PREPARE YOURSELF!

All great fiction has a crisis point. Was there a crisis point in your life that brought you to Jesus? Or not? Think about how you came to know him, or how you started on your journey. Alternatively, think of crisis points where you have prayed with passion. What kind of answer did you get? Did it improve your faith, or not? Think about your testimony – can you share it with someone this Christmas?

TO START

The next part of the film brings us to the crisis point in George's life. He's living in an old, dilapidated house that he obviously doesn't really like. He's living an 'ordinary life' like so many other people. Nothing amazing has happened to him. He hasn't even left Bedford Falls on honeymoon.

There is a very powerful lead-up to George's crisis here, when his day-to-day humdrum existence changes suddenly into something far worse.

Sometimes we take the ordinary for granted. We may even feel less than thankful most of the time. But we should live in gratitude, and this is something I often tell myself. Just stop for a moment and think of five things in your life you are truly thankful for. For me: Jesus, health, work, my mum and dad, friends, church, my home, car ... Oh, that's more than five.

One of the ways to become more thankful is to focus on Jesus and what he has done for us, and just worship. I have some favourite worship songs – I love old hymns as well as the modern ones – but at the moment, my favourite is *Revelation Song* by Jesus Culture (featuring Kim Walker-Smith). The first time I played it on YouTube, it made me cry. It tells of the awesomeness of who Jesus is. The Man they nailed to the cross is the Lord of glory. The baby who was laid in a manger, the one we look forward to coming again and celebrate during Advent – this is the King of kings, God himself, the one who said to John in Revelation 1:17-18: 'Do not be afraid. I am the First and the Last. I am the Living One; I was dead, and now look, I am alive for ever and ever! And I hold the keys of death and Hades.' Jesus holds the keys of death! And he tells us not to be afraid! Anyone who comes to him he will never turn away, as he states in John 6:37.

We can turn to him in times of trouble – but also enjoy him when times are good. You can only really trust someone you know, and know well. How do you get to know someone? Spend time with them. God doesn't want us to come to him just when we're needy, although he more than adequately provides for his children. Are you the type of Christian who has a roller coaster relationship with your heavenly Father? Close at times, but when things go well, not so close? Do you only come to him when you need something? Or alternatively, do you run away from him when things seem to take a turn for the worse?

Establishing and maintaining a close relationship with him is the answer. Read his Word, worship him, talk to him, and expect to hear from him too. Let him light up his Word for you personally; the Spirit of God illuminates the Book so it isn't a dry and dusty old text but a living Word.

And remember the Word became flesh at Christmas. He's real. He's alive. And he wants a living relationship today with *you*. The more you get to know him, the more secure you will feel and the more you will trust him. So if something comes knocking at your door that is not of God, and perhaps even something of the enemy – as 1 Peter 5:8 says, ' Be alert and of sober mind.' Why? 'Your enemy the devil prowls around like a roaring lion looking for someone to devour.' Don't let it be you! Know your Shepherd's voice so well that you won't be taken in by temptations that look good but will leave you empty – or worse. In John chapter 10, Jesus speaks about his sheep listening to and knowing his voice. Learn to discern that 'still small voice' of God (1 Kings 19:12, KJV) … and run if the enemy makes you an offer!

Pause for thought: Think about your favourite hymn/carol or worship song. Sing it/play it now!

WATCH: 1:02:19-1:02:43
George has built Bailey Park – new homes

at affordable prices for the poor people. In this clip we see Mr Martini and his family moving from a slum dwelling to a lovely new property that they will own ... courtesy of Building and Loan. The joy here is evident. And when Mary hands out the gifts, they are significant.

THINK ABOUT

1. *Bread – that this house may never know hunger*

Jesus said he was the 'bread of life' (6:35). What does this actually mean? The whole passage of John 6:25-59 is well worth a read if you have time. Bread is important; it's part of a staple diet. Jesus taught his disciples in the Lord's Prayer to ask their heavenly Father for their 'daily bread' (Matthew 6:11). Food, yes, provision, yes ... but what did Jesus mean by saying *he* was the bread?

He talks in John 6 about the manna – the bread from heaven – that God gave to the Israelites as they travelled through the desert, towards the Promised Land. (See Exodus 16.) They had to take enough manna for the day, they couldn't keep it for the next day or it would go rotten. God was teaching them to rely on him daily, and that's what we need to do in our relationship with Jesus.

Jesus said he was the bread that came down from heaven. In verse 41 he identifies himself in such a way, and the Jews questioned it. Wasn't this Jesus, 'the son of Joseph, whose father and mother we know? How can he now say, "I came down from heaven"?' (verse 42). But come from heaven he did, and that is what we remember at Advent. Born of a virgin, as the prophet Isaiah testified: 'Therefore the Lord himself will give you a sign: the virgin will conceive and give birth to a son, and will call him Immanuel', his Father was God himself. And mysteriously and wonderfully, as the prophet Micah tells us, his origins are 'from everlasting' (NKJV; NIV 1984 says in a footnote, 'from days of eternity'). At this time of Advent we might well be thinking about the mystery of the Trinity – but that is exactly what it is; the 'First and the Last' (Revelation 1:17), the 'Mighty God, Everlasting Father, Prince of Peace' (Isaiah 9:6).

But what did Jesus mean when he said that whoever ate his flesh would live forever (John 6:52)? This is what we remember in Communion, the breaking of bread – the Lord's Table. His body was broken and his blood was spilled, to make us right with God. Does that mean we literally eat Jesus' flesh? No – that's not how I read it. He said that anyone who believed in him would never hunger or thirst (John 6:35), but clearly many in our world do. It is a deeper meaning, then; a spiritual meaning. We must partake of him, that is, believe and receive his sacrifice for us, personally. And it is important to keep feeding on him daily. Keep in day-to-day contact with Jesus means developing an everyday awareness of him guiding, sustaining and leading, through his Word, through prayer and listening for his voice.

Pause for thought: Ask Jesus to fill you with his Holy Spirit. His presence can and will satisfy you.

2. *Salt – that life may always have flavour*
   Salt purifies, heals – and in this context, gives flavour. Jesus said to his followers that they were 'the salt of

the earth' (Matthew 5:13). This term in modern usage means someone who is reliable, trustworthy and so on. But here Jesus is saying that his followers give flavour. There should be something 'different' about us. Let's not become so much like the world that they don't notice any difference in us at all. The media is very influential; I believe disciples of the rabbi Jesus need to watch what we watch – as well as what we hear. We might think that in some places the Bible is old-fashioned or just plain wrong if we take on board the ideals of our culture. But sometimes a pilot has to fly by his instrumentation, not by what he sees around him. Jesus said he was the truth (John 14:6). Don't lose your saltiness – your difference! – and let that flavour your surroundings.

Pause for thought: How might you be 'salt' in your workplace or family situation this Christmas?

3. *Wine – that joy and prosperity may reign for ever*

In the Bible, wine equates with joy! Jesus turned water into wine at the wedding in Cana recorded in John 2; it was his first miracle, or 'sign'. At the wedding, the wine had run out; the joy had run out. He turned the ordinary, the everyday, into an occasion for celebration.

Joy is one of the fruits of the Holy Spirit; Galatians 5:22-23: 'love, joy, peace, forbearance, kindness, goodness, faithfulness, gentleness and self-control'. If joy is a fruit of the Spirit, then believers should show that fruit. But do we? Joy, I think, is different to 'happiness' which is largely dependent on circumstances. There is an interesting passage in 1 Peter 1:6-9: 'In all this you greatly rejoice, though now for a little while you may have had to suffer grief in all kinds of trials. These have come so that the proven genuineness of your faith ... may result in praise, glory and honour when Jesus Christ is revealed. Though you have not seen him, you love him; and ... you believe in him and are filled with an inexpressible and glorious joy, for you are receiving the end result of your faith, the salvation of your souls.' It sounds as if these people were suffering – and yet joyful. Why? Because they are 'receiving the end result' of their faith, which was salvation.

When we fix our eyes on Jesus, as we are exhorted to do in Hebrews 12:2, we begin to see things from a different perspective. Remember, the baby in the manger, the one who came to us that first Christmas, is the Lord of glory. And we will see him – one day, if we are his, we will see the beauty that is Jesus, in all his glory. Isn't that wonderful? Joy wells up within us because the Spirit lives in us, that water welling up to eternal life that Jesus spoke about in John chapter 4. This Advent, how exciting to look forward to the time when we will see him, when he comes again.

Just a quick word here about prosperity. One of the greatest heresies of today is the so-called 'prosperity gospel' – health and wealth. While Jesus can and does heal today, and his kingdom breaks in all around us as we put him first in our lives, our focus should not be on 'what he can give us'. Yes, he can prosper – and yes, he does. But let's look to our Father for himself alone, not for what he can give us. He is more than someone we can go to with a cosmic shopping list. He knows our needs.

Pause for thought: Has your joy run out? Fix your eyes on Jesus. Ask him to fill you full to overflowing!

WATCH: 1:04:48-1:09:44

The one person who isn't enjoying the prosperity brought to the poor by the altruistic efforts of George and the Building and Loan is the miserly Mr Potter. He has wanted to control it, or destroy it. But Mr Potter has a plan. He tries to tempt George, and it is a serious temptation.

Here we see him offering George everything he ever wanted. He knows George well – and he certainly knows his weaknesses. He points out all the negatives in George's life; he knows George hates his job, wants to get out on his own, feels trapped and frustrated, watching his friends move on as he stays and helps those Potter considers low-lifes. So Potter plies him with gifts and much flattery and promises him a good job, a great salary, travel to New York and Europe.

THINK ABOUT

Potter here is such a good picture of the devil and his temptations. He knows us very well, and as children of God, he desires to 'bring us down', 'take us out of the game'. He's the roaring lion from 1 Peter 5:8 but he isn't to be underestimated. We need to be aware that we are in a spiritual battle, if we belong to Jesus. Ephesians 6 makes that very plain. Here it tells us to 'be strong in the Lord and in his mighty power' (verse 10). The devil has 'schemes' (verse 11) and we are told: 'For our struggle is not against flesh and blood, but against the rulers, against the authorities, against the powers of this dark world and against the spiritual forces of evil in the heavenly realms' (verse 12). The devil has been a murderer and a liar from the beginning (John 8:44), who has come to 'steal and kill and destroy' but Jesus has come 'that [we] may have life, and have it to the full' (John 10:10).

The devil, or Satan (which means 'accuser' – see Revelation 12:10) is not the comic figure in red tights with a pitchfork that people have made him out to be. He is a real foe, with an organised force under his command. But he has been defeated by Jesus (John 12:31; John 16:11). So we need not fear but remember to 'put on the full armour of God, so that when the day of evil comes, [we] may be able to stand your ground, and after [we] have done everything, to stand' (Ephesians 6:13). Paul goes on to talk about the belt of truth, the breastplate of righteousness, feet shod with the readiness of the gospel of peace, and the shield of faith, that we might extinguish the enemy's flaming arrows; he mentions the helmet of salvation, and the word of God, the sword of the Spirit (see Ephesians 6:14-18).

George resists the temptation. Yes, he wants to get out of Bedford Falls – but not at any cost! He sees the truth of the situation, and Potter's offer for what it is; just a means by which to shut down the Building and Loan.

Jesus resisted temptation – tested as he was at the start of his ministry. We can read all about this in Matthew's gospel, chapter 4. Interestingly, although Jesus was tempted by the devil, he was led into the situation by the Spirit (see verse 1). And he passed the test; the devil tempted him three times – each time Jesus withstood him by quoting from Scripture. And that is the best way to deal with Satan's advances when he comes to tempt us. Jesus was tempted in the areas of satisfying the flesh, doubt (testing God) and power. Often, these are the areas in which we find ourselves being tempted too. If that's you today, ask God for his power to stand!

Jesus told his disciples to 'watch and pray' so they would not fall into temptation. He said the 'the spirit is willing, but the flesh is weak' (Mark 14:38); he also taught his disciples to pray: 'lead us not into temptation, but deliver us from the evil one'. When we resist temptation, we are stronger for it. But let's not go looking for it!

Pause for thought: Are you being tempted in any particular area right now? Do you need to run from it, like Joseph (see Genesis 39:12)?

WATCH: 1:11:40-1:13:13

So, George never does leave Bedford Falls. Mary has babies, and life becomes routine – until the war comes. His friends and family get involved in various ways, but George can't go to war due to his bad ear. But his brother, Harry, excels as a navy flyer – he shoots down fifteen planes, two of which were about to crash into a transport full of soldiers.

THINK ABOUT

Illness, when it is long-lasting, can be debilitating. I remember when I had Ménière's disease, looking out of my window watching people living their ordinary lives. Old age, too, can be isolating, when people feel that others are 'out, doing' and the older person can only be 'home, sitting'. I have a friend, in her forties, who has severe Crohn's disease and her life has been very affected by her illness. She can't work, and is exhausted much of the time. But a couple of years ago, she started to follow Jesus. And although she can't do very much, her home is full of the peace of that presence. I think sometimes Jesus challenges us that he has plenty of people who want to 'work' for him, but not so many who want to 'be' with him. When you are in love with someone, you just want to be with them, don't you? When I was unable to work or do anything much, I prayed, telling him that I only ever wanted to work for him. And yet I saw that it wasn't so much about 'working for him' as letting him do *his* work in me. Resting in God is an important lesson to learn. Resting isn't always our choice, of course. But when we do choose to rest – inwardly – we will find ourselves enjoying more of his presence, and ultimately, serving him in greater ways.

> *Pause for thought: Have you ever felt 'left behind'?*

WATCH: 1:15:53-1:17:46; 1:20:17-1:21:03

It's the day before Christmas. And it's all over the papers – Harry has won the Congressional Medal of Honor. George's mother has had lunch with the President's wife!

Full of pride and excitement about Harry's achievements, Uncle Billy can't help showing off to Mr Potter in the bank, as he gone to deposit $8,000 worth of cash for the Building and Loan. But in his delight, boasting to his enemy, he inadvertently slips the envelope of money inside Potter's newspaper – and Mr Potter, on finding it, is certainly not going to let Billy know he has it.

Mr Carter, the bank examiner, is at the

Building and Loan. So is Violet – a woman now of questionable character, and George is helping her.

The loss of the money soon becomes apparent, and George loses his temper with his distressed and distraught uncle. He yells that this means 'bankruptcy and scandal and prison'. George has snapped.

A moment's carelessness, and a devastating result!

THINK ABOUT

How easy it is to lose something precious, when we don't handle it with care: Relationships, friendships – anything – we need to treasure them. One moment of skating where we should not skate – it's that icy dip again.

Pause for thought: Have you ever done something you regret, that has hurt you or someone else? Can you put it right? Ask God to help you.

WATCH: 1:21:16-1:28:28

This is a long clip, but an important one as we see the increasing strain George Bailey is under. He's on the edge of a breakdown. At home, with the repetitive strains of 'Hark! The Herald Angels Sing' in a monotonous background, being pounded out on the piano by one of his daughters, George slowly unravels. Everything comes to a head. He loses his temper with the kids, berates Mary with why they 'have to live here in the first place and stay around this measly crummy old town', questions whether they are a happy family, as he asks, 'Why do we have to have all these kids' although his love for them is evident, as he pretends to 'paste' his daughter Zuzu's flower, hiding the petals in his pocket. He destroys a model of a bridge that he has obviously been constructing at home, symbolic of destroying all his dreams forever. Along with his irritation for the children, he even attacks their teacher and her husband verbally on the phone.

But watch this – Mary and the children know what to do. Prayer, they know, is the answer. As this is suggested by one of the children, Janie, who has been castigated for playing the carol, it is all the more poignant.

THINK ABOUT
Jesus requires us to have the faith of a child (Matthew 18:3-4). What does this mean?

Child-like doesn't mean childish. As a child trusts a good and loving father, and comes to him unafraid with all its needs, so we must trust our Father God.

Sadly, Christmas and the run-up to it is well-known as a stressful period, and a time when tempers can fray. A friend of mine used to work for a letting agency, and she said that January was their busiest month – letting out bedsits and flats to people when their relationships broke down during and after the Christmas break.

Living in a troubled house with parents – or step-parents – who don't get on, are under pressure financially and in other ways, can be very hard indeed for everyone concerned, but especially the children. In a time where families don't seem to stay together as they used to, many children find they are spending the Christmas season with parents who are no longer living together. 'Blended families' are not always easy to negotiate, and grandparents can miss out if children are no longer living with their offspring. There are plenty of adults too who are still affected by their childhood 'broken homes'.

Pause for thought: Spend a few minutes praying for anyone you know who is going through a hard time in their marriage – or for any children you know who are suffering because of parental break-up.

WATCH: 1:28-32-1:30:50

In his desperation, George turns to the one person he thinks can help him. Sadly, the person he turns to first is more than happy to make the most of his adversary's misfortune ... and gets a kick out of it. George begs Mr Potter for help, after explaining that the Building and Loan are short in their accounts; they have misplaced $8,000. Potter, of course, knows *exactly* why they are short, and yet gleefully goads and mocks him. George hasn't notified the police because of Harry's imminent homecoming, and is truly at the mercy of his enemy.

Potter takes full advantage of the situation to slander George's character – has he been playing the market with the company's money, or is there a woman involved? He mentions Violet ...

How Potter enjoys George's misery!

What a picture of gloating unforgiveness and sheer evil intent.

The only security George has is his life insurance ... as Potter says, he is worth more dead than alive.

THINK ABOUT

To turn someone away when they need help, even an enemy, in such a desperate situation, and get such pleasure from it as Potter seems to, is a picture of absolutely the wrong sort of 'joy'. When he offered George the chance of a job earlier, it was out of no kind motive. That's apparent. There's no love here – not even ordinary human kindness! What a picture of evil. The devil may tempt us, he may offer us greatness. Let's not make the mistake of ever thinking there is kindness at the root, or that he is offering anything for our good and our benefit.

I wonder, is there anyone in your life that you are holding a grudge against? Someone who hurt you, maybe even years ago, someone that you'd like to 'get your own back' on, if at all possible? Someone you wouldn't help, even if they begged you? We have already discussed the importance of forgiveness in this book. Jesus said we should love our enemies and pray for the ones who persecute us (see Matthew 5:43-47). That's really hard, almost impossible to do, in our own strength. But we have to remember that we forgive so that we might be forgiven (Matthew 6:14-15; see also Matthew 18:21-35). When we see the sins of others, we need to remember that we ourselves are in no way perfect. Forgiveness sets us free, too; you can't move forward while you are looking back, chained to a person and an event that you can't change. Unforgiveness and bitterness only hurts us, in the end. And forgiving someone isn't really 'letting them off the hook' as they will stand before God one day; it is instead, letting ourselves off the hook. Jesus forgave his enemies from the cross (Luke 23:34). Let's leave our enemies in God's hands, but extend grace to them if we can – even if it just means praying a blessing on them. We don't necessarily have to see them – anyway, at times we are unable to, or it might not be wise or safe to do so.

But let's just make sure, shall we, that we are never among the 'Mr Potters' of this world.

Pause for thought: Do you think Mr Potter has any redeeming feature?

WATCH: 1:31:39-1:33:24

Here we come to the crisis point in the film. George is in Martini's bar, as Potter has called for a warrant for his arrest. And George prays the kind of prayer we pray when we really don't know what to say. It's the prayer of many who have never met Jesus for themselves, who don't know him, who are not 'praying men' or 'praying women'. But at a time of crisis, they call out to God.

George says: 'God ... Dear Father in heaven ...' and begins by saying he is not a praying man, but if God is up there, and can hear him, will he show him the way? He truly is at the end of his rope ...

Sadly, the answer to his prayer seems to be a punch in the face from the teacher's husband he has shouted at earlier. Is that really what you get for praying?

THINK ABOUT

I know of stories of people who have been in the direst of circumstances and have cried out to a God who has shown himself to them. When I was in my twenties I was anxious, unhappy, had lost a business, one of my closest friends had been found dead, and my parents had divorced. At that low point, I cried out to Jesus, 'If you're really there, you handle my life, because I can't handle it anymore.' I knew something had changed, immediately. No angelic choirs or anything, but a sense of peace – and joy. I went downstairs and my mother remarked, 'What's happened to you? You're smiling!' That was the start of my walk with Jesus.

There are people who have been far more 'down' than I, and yet Jesus has lifted them up when they called out to him. Drug addicts, prostitutes, criminals – I have met many people who have found Jesus in the depths of their despair.

In the movie at this point, our hero has greatly changed from the young boy, upbeat and cheerful, full of hopes and dreams. Life has broken him. But George is calling out for help now from the one who really can help him. The one who will not turn him away, or scorn his plea for help. One that will not rejoice in his downfall, but one who is more than eager to assist. And that's where the next chapter will begin.

> *Pause for thought: Have you ever cried out to God in desperation, and found him in the brokenness?*

ADVENT CONNECTION

READ: LUKE 1:5-25; LUKE 2:22-38

Here we read the stories of the 'co-stars' in the Advent story. Elizabeth and her husband, Zechariah, are old, and have no children. Zechariah is a priest, a holy man, and on going in the temple to burn incense to the Lord, he encounters an angel who says his wife will bear a child. Zechariah, possibly jaded, doesn't believe him, and is unable to speak until the child is born – just as the angel says. In Luke 1:14, the angel Gabriel says that the child will be 'a joy and delight' to his parents. He speaks of John the Baptist, the forerunner of the Messiah, Jesus.

The most interesting part of these readings for me is the second reading, where we meet another devout man, Simeon, who had been promised by the Spirit of God that he would not see death until he had seen the Messiah. He gave a prophecy to Mary – that Jesus would 'cause the falling and rising of many in Israel' and would be 'a sign that will be spoken against' (verse 34), and that 'the thoughts of many hearts [would] be revealed' (verse 35). In that verse he also revealed that 'a sword [would] pierce [Mary's] own soul too' – just as a sword pierced the side of her son on the cross. He called Jesus a 'light' for those who did not know God; a light shows the way. It is fascinating to read that Simeon says that now he can depart this life in peace; once you have seen Jesus, everything is different. There was also an elderly prophetess in the temple, Anna, possibly an overlooked and forgotten woman, who told all the people of the child she had seen.

These people were not 'main players' in Jesus' story, like Mary and Joseph. But their lives were unquestionably changed by the coming of Jesus. And how joyful they must have been, as God touched their lives at this time, giving them new hope!

Life may be tough for us; it might be that this Advent season is a particularly difficult one for you. Perhaps you are living with huge amounts of stress; financial crisis; a bad report from the doctor; perhaps you are going through a family break-up. (If your partner – or you yourself – is feeling the strain and showing any kinds of physical symptoms, including verbal or other kinds of abuse, I'd urge you to seek help – now.) If you are in any kind of crisis situation, call out to God – call to him from your heart. Phone or visit a trusted Christian friend, if you can, to share your situation.

In the middle of it all, let's remember what we are really celebrating at Christmas. I hope you are joyful in your expectation, but if you aren't, think about what Advent *really* means. It's the coming of a King. But it is also the coming of a Saviour. As I first read in Watchman Nee's excellent *Sit, Walk, Stand* (CLC), when someone is drowning, you can't leap in and rescue them until they are exhausted. If you do, you will find yourself dragged down with them. But if you wait until they have stopped struggling, you may be able to jump in and save them. God is like that – he waits until we are desperate enough to call out to him, when we realise we can't save ourselves.

But think too of the joy that is available to us, when we know we are loved by our Saviour! He has come into the world, why?

To make us right with God, why? Because we needed a Saviour, we could not save ourselves. That is how much we are loved by our wonderful God! He isn't a miserly Mr Potter character, waiting for us to fail so he can give us an even tougher time. No. He's the father in the story of the prodigal son, waiting for us to return, and then rushing to clothe us with his love and acceptance (see Luke 15:11-31). He forgives, completely, when we turn to him. And he is the perfect one – the one we are all answerable to. But he doesn't hold a grudge. Instead, he gives, and gives, and gives – hope, peace, joy, love. But the inexpressible joy that comes from knowing that whatever our circumstances, whatever our situation – we have a hope and future in Jesus, the Faithful One, the one we can trust our lives and ultimate safety to, because he loves us – loves us enough to die for us. He is raised from the dead, and seated at the right hand of his Father. And he knows and loves *you*.

Pause for thought
- Sometimes we can waver in our faith, when we pray and seem to

receive no answer – or things just get worse. God hears prayers, but he always shows the pray-er to his Son. If we really want to know God, we need to come to him through Jesus. Why?

- There's not much joy in George's Christmas so far. Indeed, there's not much joy in his life at all. Do you understand that Christian joy is not dependent on circumstances – how real is that for you? (Be honest!)

ACTIVITY SUGGESTIONS:

- Find some bread, salt and wine (or juice). Spend some time reflecting on what these three items represent, in regards to the Bible. How do you think God may be speaking to you as you contemplate each item? (For example: As bread sustains our bodies, so Jesus, the Bread of Life, sustains our very life; what does that mean for you?)

- Do you have any friends, relatives or neighbours who you know are finding this Christmas difficult? Can you do anything to ease their stress? If it's you, is there anything you can do to relieve your own pressures? For example, make a list of things you don't actually need to do!

REFLECTION:

'Do not be afraid. I bring you good news that will cause great joy for all the people.' So said the angel in Luke 2:10. As we get nearer to the day itself, meditate on this verse when you can. Which part of it speaks most to you – don't be afraid? I bring you good news? Great joy?

PRAYER

Dear heavenly Father, it's so easy to forget you in the middle of the stress of our lives this Advent season, and to forget that it's your coming, Jesus, that we are celebrating! Let it be all about you, Lord. Help me to let go of what I need to let go of. And trust. And rest, on the inside. Amen.

CHAPTER FOUR
THE RIGHT PERSPECTIVE

PREPARE YOURSELF!

Review your life! Think about the people you have known who have influenced you for good. Perhaps it is someone who has shown you Jesus in their lifestyle, or even introduced you to him. And think of the people that *you* have influenced or helped along the way. If you have children, or grandchildren, praise God for them; they wouldn't be here if it wasn't for you!

TO START

As Christmas approaches, you may find less time to spend on this devotional, as you are caught up with wrapping the last presents and trying to tick off various items of foods – and relatives – on any list you may have! But do try to view the clips at some point during the holiday. They are such a blessing.

At times we have to get a different perspective on things to see them clearly. Where I live, there are two churches, one at the top of the hill and one at the bottom. From a certain viewpoint, they look very close together and level. But that's a skewed perspective. We often have that, don't we? But God sees things as they really are.

As Christians, it is a very releasing and freeing thing to see who we are in Christ. When we surrender to him, give our lives to him, we begin to realise that in some mysterious way, he has chosen us. In John 15:16 Jesus says: 'You did not choose me, but I chose you and appointed you so that you might go and bear fruit – fruit that will last'. The Father has lavished *his* love on us; we could never seat ourselves in the heavenly realms, but that is what he has done for those who are in Christ: 'because of his great love for us, God, who is rich in mercy, made us alive with Christ even when we were dead in transgressions – it is by grace you have been saved. And God raised us up with Christ and seated us with him in the heavenly realms in Christ Jesus' (Ephesians 2:4-6; if you have time after Christmas is over, read through Ephesians 1 and 2).

In the final clips of *It's a Wonderful Life*, we see what a difference a change of perspective makes to our beleaguered hero. And what a difference he has made to the lives of others. I think maybe we don't realise how many lives our own life has touched; and we don't realise, either, what we have until it looks as if we may not have it any longer. How many of us regret a 'grass is greener' attitude, where we may have forfeited something for something (or someone) else, and now realise that what we had before was – well, just fine? There's a saying, isn't there, that we only miss something (or somebody) when we no longer have it (or them)!

As human beings, we seem to long for what we don't have. We're a bit like the Israelites, wandering in the desert, complaining about the food they'd known in captivity and in so doing rubbishing the freedom they had been given, and negating the goodness of God (see Numbers 11:4-6).

At this time of year, it is easy to focus on the material world, what we have and what we haven't got. But the acquisition for more 'stuff' is not what life is all about. In the end, it's who you know, not what you've got that matters. Does chasing after worldly wealth ever make anyone truly happy? We always want more and more ... and yet, today's new car is tomorrow's scrap.

The apostle Paul speaks about being content in our current circumstances (see Philippians 4:11-12; 1 Timothy 6:7-9; Hebrews 13:5). Not always easy to do, but it *is* always right to praise God for who he is, and maintain an attitude of thankfulness. Philippians 4:4-7 says: 'Rejoice in the Lord always. I will say it again: rejoice! Let your gentleness be evident to all. The Lord is near. Do not be anxious about anything, but in every situation, by prayer and petition, with thanksgiving, present your requests to God. And the peace of God, which transcends all understanding, will guard your hearts and your minds in Christ Jesus.'

Before you start to watch the next clip, why not stop, and thank God for the way in which he has blessed you? He loves us so much he sent his Son – that's why we are journeying through Advent!

Pause for thought: Count your blessings ... they may number more than you imagine.

WATCH: 1:34:27-1:35:35; 1:35:41-1:37:01; 1:37:34-1:39:43

Note: You may wish to watch this section as a whole. Alternatively, watch it in three sections, as indicated above.

In the first of these clips, we see George contemplating suicide by drowning. And we see him being rescued in a very unlikely way as an elderly man (who we later find out is Clarence, the angel) jumps into the water first – which of course makes George dive in to save him! Even in his toughest hour, George thinks of others first; something we can see that the angel expected, because this is George's known character.

Skipping on a little bit, the second clip is a revealing one. The guardian angel reveals who he is. I think we have to suspend the differences in the film's artistic licence and our biblical understanding of angels here. As we explored above, angels aren't dead people (and neither do they win their wings by earning them, just as we can do nothing to earn our own salvation).

George mentions that he got a thump in the jaw in answer to prayer. And then Clarence says *he* is the answer to the prayer. He has been sent from heaven.

THINK ABOUT

In the book of Daniel, we see an angel being sent in answer to a prayer – and he was delayed for some time (see Daniel 10:12-13). Spiritual resistance delayed the answer! Sometimes we feel we have prayed and prayed and that God doesn't hear us. There might be a delay, a hindrance, or answers may not come as we expect. But he *does* hear us.

In the clip we hear that suicide is against the law both where George lives, and in heaven too. We don't have time here to discuss suicide and how God views it. Suffice it to say that to want to take your own life, you must be in a place many of us cannot begin to imagine. God made each of us, and he values our lives so much that he sent his Son to die so we can live. There is hope in Jesus and in a God who loves us and understands our very hearts. No situation is ever hopeless, once Jesus is involved – this is the Man who raised the dead when all hope seemed lost. If we are ever in a situation where we feel that no one can help, and nothing can change – we need to turn it all over to the Sovereign One who loves us.

In the third clip, we listen in on the

conversation George has with Clarence. If it hadn't been for him, thinks George, his wife and children and friends would be a lot better off. Indeed, it would have been better if he had never been born at all ...

Which sparks a life-turning event for George Bailey!

Pause for thought: Have you been waiting for an answer to prayer, and are losing hope that God has heard you?

WATCH: 1:44:24-1:47:35

Here Clarence and George are in what turns out to be Nick's bar (not Martini's). But it is a very different Nick to the friend George has known; this version is tough and brutal.

Clarence asks an interesting question: If people believe in angels, why are they surprised when they see one? And George, embarrassed, responds that he has never grown up ... an interesting aside. Do we feel belief in the supernatural is not acceptable, once we are adults?

Mr Gower comes in, but he isn't the Mr Gower George has known before. He is a broken, shambling wreck of a man, despised and humiliated; he has spent twenty years in prison for poisoning a child – because George wasn't there to stop him from putting the poison into the capsules.

Things have changed. People have changed. And George is beginning to see just how different the world would have been without him …

WATCH: 1:48:10-1:55:16

This is a long clip, but worth sitting down and watching because it gives some an authentic atmosphere of change and desolation. Without George to stop him, Potter has taken over Bedford Falls. It is now called Pottersville! Prohibitive signs litter the place – and it is a crude, rough, dissolute town; a town manifestly lacking in love and goodwill. Building and Loan went out of business years go. Nobody knows George. Violet has become a lost soul; his friend the taxi driver, Ernie, lives in a shack, not in the lovely Bailey Park, and his wife has left him.

George's home – the draughty old house he so despised – is a ruin. And there are no children …

His mother is running a boarding house.

What a different woman 'Ma Bailey' seems, hard and cold and jaded! And George finds out that his Uncle Billy has been in the insane asylum ever since he lost his business.

Clarence points out that it is strange how one life touches so many other lives. And when a person isn't around, they certainly leave a gap.

Bailey Park is a cemetery; after all, George wasn't there to build the houses. And in that cemetery George finds his brother Harry's grave; he died when he fell through the ice at the age of nine – George wasn't there to rescue him. Consequently there was no Harry Bailey to go to war, so every soldier on the transport died because Harry wasn't there to save them.

As Clarence points out, George really did have a wonderful life. What a mistake it would be to throw it away!

The clip ends with Mary as an 'old maid', nervous and plain, not the vibrant, joyful woman George had married.

THINK ABOUT

Have you ever thought about how much your life has touched that of other people's? This film made me think about it. I have been thinking too about how the lives of others have affected me. I once bought a book that changed my life. *I Dared to Call Him Father* by Bilquis Sheikh (Kingsway) presented me with a woman who knew Jesus as her friend, and I realised that if it was possible, I wanted that too. I gave my life to Christ shortly afterwards. So Bilquis was highly significant in my coming to Jesus. Sometimes we touch people for Christ and don't know it. That can be a very useful thing to remember, especially when we are involved in evangelism and have prayed perhaps for years for individuals, and have not seen an answer – as yet. If that's you, don't give up. You don't know how your life, your words, your prayers, your smallest witness has affected people!

But of course, although we can influence lives for good, there are times when we have hurt others, and others have hurt us. We explored the issue of forgiveness earlier, but if you still struggle in this area, put this book down for a moment and bring any residual pain and hurt before God.

By the way, being unmarried, and believing that this is God's 'Plan A' right now, I'm not sure how I feel about the 'old maid' scene. I have friends who have never married, and I wonder how they might view the negative portrayal of singledom here, too! Still, it's a film of its time.

Pause for thought: Make a date (perhaps in the less stressful New Year) to contact someone who has influenced you for Christ, to thank and encourage them.

WATCH: 1:56:22-1:56:59

George has escaped from the nightmare of Pottersville to the bridge where he was going to kill himself. His short excursion into a different reality has made a huge difference to him. Seeing how much he has thrown away, he just wants to get back to his wife and children. He cries out that he wants to live again: 'Please God, let me live again.'

THINK ABOUT

Crying out to Clarence doesn't work. But crying out to God does, as we see as we come to the end of this wonderful film. Only God can answer our heart's cry. No angel, no person can do it. St Augustine is well-known to have said: 'Thou hast made us for thyself, O Lord, and our heart is restless until it finds its rest in thee.' And it *does* find its rest in him. God knows our hearts. He knows your desperate cry just as he knows mine. And he wants us to 'live again' – a fresh, new life, lived in his power. Do you know him?

Pause for thought: You may have called on people, or alternative spiritual realities – but today, call on the name of Jesus.

WATCH: 1:57:57-2:02

Although by now it is very likely that Christmas is upon you, if you have the time, settle down and watch the heart-warming end of this amazing film with a mince pie, or some of your favourite snacks. What a different George Bailey we see here! He is delighted to see Bedford Falls. He even wishes the 'wonderful old Building and Loan' a merry Christmas! I noticed that he wishes Mr Potter a happy Christmas – a new perspective has made him love his enemy!

The people he most wants to see,

understandably, are his family. How he loves his children, and his wife! There is great rejoicing. But what of the missing money? Well, all the people he has helped rally to his aid; what a miracle! All give sacrificially, including Violet! They give as generously to him as he has given to them.

THINK ABOUT

I couldn't help but think about Jesus' words in Matthew 7:2 here. 'With the measure you use, it will be measured to you.' George has given his life to Bedford Falls, at the cost of his dreams. What a life of self-sacrifice! And although he considered it wasted, he now sees that it wasn't at all. Jesus said: 'Whoever tries to keep their life will lose it, and whoever loses their life will preserve it' (Luke 17:33). To follow him is a sacrifice. It means taking up our cross *daily* and denying ourselves if we want to be disciples of Jesus (see Luke 9:23). That's a hard one, isn't it? We so often want our own way. And yet, to live God's way is ultimately the most rewarding of all.

I was thinking about the feeding of the 5,000 recently (see John 6:1-14) and I wondered: the little boy gave all he had to Jesus – a few small loaves and fish – and it must have seemed so inadequate to the task at hand. But these few items were all the child had to eat, so it was a sacrifice for him to give it up. Sometimes it is hard to let go of something we want to hold onto, when Jesus asks us to do so. But when we are willing, he will often either give it back to us in some form, or give us something better. The fact is, Jesus wants our full devotion. And he will challenge us to let go of anything that we love more than him.

George Bailey has given his life to serve people – and it is truly a wonderful life. He has lost his life, so to speak, but by the end of the film sees that he has actually lost nothing at all. Selfish living could have provided no greater reward than the love with which he is surrounded.

Pause for thought: Thank God for the love of friends and family.

WATCH: 2:03:00–2:03:44

With the arrival of Harry, the happy ending is complete. Harry toasts his brother as 'the richest man in town'. This resonates as true for George in a way that Harry cannot know.

Harry is alive, the family is intact. George, we know, feels a lot more than mere gratitude. As the film ends, we know that the rest of his life will be lived from a different viewpoint. It's only when we think we may have lost something precious that we see how blessed we truly are.

Love reigns. Love is the important thing. The copy of the book left to him by Clarence states: 'Remember no man is a failure who has friends.' George wanted to build things, but by putting his own desires second, he built into people's lives and accomplished far more than he had dreamed.

THINK ABOUT

Through this Advent season, and Christmas-time with all its wrong focus on the material world, at the end of it all, love is what matters most. Love *for* others. Love *from* others. Let's remember that the divine love that came down from heaven to rescue us when we didn't know we needed rescuing, is the greatest love of all.

In John 15 Jesus calls us his friends if we do what he commands. What does he want us to do? Obey him. How do we obey him?

Verse 12 is clear. We must love each other. How? As he has loved us. That means sacrificially (see verse 13). It's easy to love those who love us back, but not always so easy to love those who are difficult, and certainly not to love those who have hurt us in some way. But maybe, as we look at our lives afresh with George Bailey, we can each say that when we realise what we have, and what Jesus has done for us, it is not impossible to let go of past hurts and trust God for the future, as we remember that nothing can separate us from the love of God that is in Jesus (Romans 8:35-39).

To love God wholeheartedly is the first commandment. Flowing from that comes a love for others (see Matthew 22:37-40). When we understand how much God has loved us, we too can be free to live a life of grace, freedom and love. In 1 Corinthians, we read that out of faith, hope and love, the greatest is love – 'Love never fails' (verse 8). God himself is love (1 John 4:8). And that is how we know that God will never, *ever*, fail us.

Pause for thought: What (and who) are you most grateful for, this Christmas?

ADVENT CONNECTION

READ: MATTHEW 2

Although the visit of the Magi, or Wise Men, happened sometime after Jesus' birth, it is often included in traditional nativity scenes. They come bearing their gifts – gold (for a King); frankincense (for deity) and myrrh (symbolising death). Interestingly, in Revelation 5:8 the 'prayers of the saints' is likened to incense. If you are a believer, you are a 'saint', as the New Testament readily asserts. So be assured, if you know Jesus, your prayers are heard.

The Magi come from the east, possibly Persia, or modern-day Iran. These stargazers had seen a sign in the sky that a King had been born, and they have come to find him. But he is not to be found where they expected. He isn't in a palace. No; he is by this time in an ordinary dwelling, after being born in an outhouse because there was no room for him anywhere else.

King Herod naturally sees the new King as a threat to his own dominion. He discovers that the Messiah will be born in

Bethlehem – that is prophesised (verse 6). The king tells the Magi that he wants to worship the Messiah too, so instructs them to return when they have found him. But it's a trick, and the Magi obey a warning given to them in a dream not to return to Herod. Herod, furious, plans to destroy the child – and what an evil plan it is, to kill all the boys in Bethlehem of two years and under – but the Saviour escapes his clutches.

The Magi found something special where they didn't expect it to be. They found something extraordinary in the ordinary.

Finding Jesus – the extraordinary in the ordinary – gives us a fresh start. Do we expect to find almighty God as a helpless baby, born into a poor family, growing up to be a carpenter, who mixed with 'sinners' and was nailed to a cross? Pure love … Is that who we think God is?

We may not have found him through an angelic visit, or chorus, in a temple, or by a guiding star. We may have found him as someone else told us about him – or by reading a book. However we have found him, when we do, we begin 'to live again', a new life, lived in his power.

How about you? Have you found him? If not, this Christmas, why not let him find you?

Pause for thought
- Do you agree that 'no man is a failure who has friends'?

- Do you expect to find something extraordinary in the ordinary – in your own life, for example?

ACTIVITY SUGGESTIONS:

- In the film, George's daughter is playing 'Hark! The Herald Angels Sing'. This carol has wonderful, strong lyrics. Read them online, or sing the song out loud!

- Read through 1 Corinthians 13, and thank God for those you love, and who love you.

REFLECTION:

George Bailey doesn't only see the good he has accomplished in his self-sacrifice, but he also sees what life would have been like if he hadn't been born. When we surrender ourselves to Jesus, he will build something far more beautiful into our lives than we could ever imagine, or expect. One day we may be surprised at how God's 'Plan A' really was the best, even if we struggled to see it. Perhaps this is the time to surrender your life anew to Jesus – to live again, in him?

PRAYER

Father God, thank you for my whole life. Thank you for the gift of love. Thank you most of all for loving us so much that you sent your Son to die on the cross to take away our sins so we can be right with you. Thank you for the new life you promise those who come to your Son. I want to live again, Lord! Amen.

CONCLUSION

So we come to the end of our journey with *It's a Wonderful Life*, a film packed with thought-provoking and challenging scenes, and a plot that speaks to us all, for we all want to feel loved and valued, and of some significance. We need to feel as if we *matter*; as if our very existence makes a difference, however small. We need to know, deep down, that our life has a purpose and a meaning, after all.

I have mentioned how I think the world's fantasy 'Christmas' promises much but delivers little. Yet, if we keep our eyes on Jesus, and remember the real reason why we are celebrating, I believe we can find the Advent season rewarding, and will maybe be able to look back and remember it as a time when we found the hope, peace, joy and love that has come from above.

I have walked with Jesus for many years. I've ignored his gentle advice and selfishly gone my own way at times, but I have also known the joy of a Shepherd who comes to the rescue, who never leaves me, who is always faithful, who extends grace when I don't deserve it, and who is ever-willing to give me a fresh start.

I don't know your situation. It could be that you have known Jesus for a long time, and that the walk has become difficult, or you could even be a little disillusioned. Maybe your cross is getting hard to bear. Perhaps, with George Bailey, you need to review your life from a different perspective, and ask Jesus for freshness in your journey – a new revelation of him – because you want 'to live again' rather than go through what may have become a dreary religious routine. Or perhaps you have not followed him closely, or at all; maybe now is the time to begin a new life. You only have to ask him. As we consider the shepherds, Mary, the devout people in the temple, the Magi, we see that God reaches out to the outcasts, the rejected, the young, the old, the jaded, the forgotten, the spiritual seekers – no one is excluded from the invitation to come to him. But remember, reviewing your past is one thing – but the past, while a good place to visit once in a while, is not a good place to live.

As a new year dawns, and this Christmas is relegated to the past, along with discarded trees and wrapping paper, try to recall the scenes from this film that have meant the most to you, and how God has spoken to you through them. Although the relatives have all gone home, Jesus remains. He didn't stay as a baby in a manger; he grew up, he showed us what God is like, died for you and for me, and rose from the dead, proving he really is who he said he was.

As we realise how much we have to be grateful for, even if life is tough, we can look forward to a wonderful future, when we believe in him. 2 Corinthians 4:17 tells us that 'our light and momentary troubles are achieving for us an eternal glory that far outweighs them all'. Let's remember that Jesus said that whoever lives and believes in him will never die (John 11:25). This world is not all there is. So let's fix our eyes on the eternal unseen.

In Revelation 3:20 the risen Christ says: 'Here I am! I stand at the door and knock. If anyone hears my voice and opens the door, I will come in and eat with that person, and they with me.' He wants intimate fellowship with each one of us. His first coming made that possible, and his second Advent surely can't be far away. Jesus comes to live with us in our ordinary lives, and makes them extraordinary.

Do you want to live again, and have a wonderful life with Jesus? I know I do!

IDEAS FOR GROUPS

1. If you have decided to share this Advent journey with some friends, I suggest you play the whole film one evening, with some Christmas nibbles. Chat about the film in general, using some of the *Pause for thought* pieces above. You might like to choose the pieces you want to explore further, and pause the movie at points indicated. Have a relaxed evening (or afternoon), but make sure relevant points (such as dealing with disappointment, greed, temptation, un/answered prayer/ different perspectives) are explored.

2. Alternatively, ask the group to think about the following discussion points:

   • Can we learn to trust God through suffering and disappointment?

- Is it ever right to act on the statement: 'I want to do what I want to do!'?

- 'All that you can take with you is that which you have given away.' True or false?

- What does it mean to you to want 'to live again'?

Then arrange to meet on a separate night (perhaps the following week) and ask your group what their thoughts have been about the film since they viewed it. Which of the discussion points has resonated most with them, and why? Or has God been speaking to them from other areas of the film? Share openly and honestly, and offer prayer (or further help) to anyone who desires it. Remind them that this is a film about perspectives. Hopefully, this will be a chance to develop further intimacy with God and each other.

3. A third idea, if you would prefer a more structured and traditional look at the Advent themes here, would be to view the film, and concentrate on the 'Advent

Connection' sections. You may play the film, then arrange meetings where your group looks at 1) Hope: who Jesus actually is; 2) Peace: Mary, who acted out of faith, not fear; 3) Joy: how Jesus changes any life he touches; 4) Love: as God becomes Man, we discover the extraordinary where we do not expect it.

For each of the above, you can use the 'Prepare Yourself!' ideas as icebreakers, or base starter discussions around them.